Grand Memories

**The Life and Times of the
Grand Theatre and Opera House, Leeds**

Patricia Lennon & David Joy

GREAT NORTHERN

Great Northern Books
PO Box 213, Ilkley, LS29 9WS
www.greatnorthernbooks.co.uk

ISBN: 1 905080 20 4

Design and layout: David Burrill

Printed by Quebecor Ibérica, Barcelona

CIP Data
A catalogue for this book is available from the British Library

CONTENTS

The authors and the publishers would like to thank the following for their help in the preparation of this book: Warren Smith and Margaret Ashbee, respectively General Manager and Marketing Manager of Leeds Grand Theatre & Opera House; Richard Ashton of Opera North; Leeds Amateur Operatic Society; Northern Ballet Theatre; Leodis Collection, Library and Information Service, Leeds City Council; West Yorkshire Archive Service; Yorkshire Post Newspapers.

FOREWORD

Most of my early memories of theatre are associated with the Grand in Leeds. Originally, I suppose it was pantomime in the early 1930s, something I looked forward to every Christmas holidays as a major pleasure, with its new takes each year on much of the action, and always with one or even two major comics in the cast. Later my brother and I graduated to plays, and saw most of the pre-London efforts which used to occupy the Grand pretty regularly. Those were mixed with occasional performances of ballet and even opera.

Wartime brought an even more regular supply of new plays and occasional revivals destined for London, and we caught them all. The Grand is rather big for spoken drama but that never occurred to us sixty years ago. Actors were not restricted then by an imaginary microphone and they projected into the theatre with no difficulty at all. That is not so regularly the case nowadays and it seems to take a Donald Sinden to give the audience the full treatment which was regular in the past.

Of course for me the Grand assumed a new and greater significance with the decision arrived at by the Arts Council and Leeds City Council together putting the theatre at the disposal of what after a year or two became Opera North. It was a complicated situation, arrived at by a simple exercise of imagination. English National Opera, of which I was Managing Director, customarily toured in late winter and early spring to appropriate theatres out of London. This was part of our agreement with the Arts Council and it was easy when a number of productions revived at the Coliseum had been designed originally for Sadler's Wells, a much smaller theatre and one whose sets fitted into theatres all over the country. As these productions were faded out and new and much grander ones put in their place, it became harder and harder to find theatres which could accommodate them. I made representations to the Arts Council that our touring was grinding to a halt, both artistically and financially.

Finally, they agreed and recommended to Leeds that the Grand Theatre, which had reverted to ownership by the city, would make a perfect place for a new venture and would at the same time enhance the standing of Leeds as a city of culture.

I think I must pull a couple of names out of a fairly well filled hat in this connection. Bernard Atha spearheaded Leeds's theatrical moves and he was in favour of this one. The Arts Council's initiative was headed by Jack Phipps, who ran their touring and believed that the foundation of a new company, run by ENO but eventually with its own distinct identity, could solve the touring problem, in not only a satisfactory but a highly constructive manner. Many other people helped to found the new company in the great old theatre, and the art form itself benefited just as surely as did the city.

We used to discuss the theatre's shortcomings, which were mostly associated with an inexorable advance into shabbiness, but nobody was brave enough to take the decision to undertake the expensive but necessary refurbishment. Finally, this has been brought about, again by a mixture of imagination and financial expertise, and the future should see not only an enhanced Grand Theatre but also an updated investment in the surrounding area.

I look forward to this future not only with anticipation but even with confidence.

Lord Harewood

THE FIRST HUNDRED YEARS

FIRST STEPS

It was an apparently off-the-cuff remark by Prince Albert, Queen Victoria's consort, which inspired the building of the Grand Theatre. When the Queen and her consort visited Leeds in 1858 to open the Town Hall, Albert reputedly commented to the mayor that Leeds seemed in need of a good theatre as 'nothing was more calculated to promote culture and raise the tone of the people'. They were words that foreshadowed the tendency of royal consorts to court controversy, as it was a time when many pious Nonconformists feared what was described as the 'insidious influence of theatrical entertainments'.

Nevertheless, they inspired a group of Leeds worthies to propose the erection of what in the grandiose phraseology of the time was described as 'a magnificent temple of drama for the West Riding'. Even though Leeds did not become a city until 1893, it was enjoying a period of phenomenal expansion. Yet progress was slow until 1875 when by an extraordinary coincidence both the existing theatres in Leeds were destroyed by fire within the space of nine months. The loss of the Theatre Royal in Hunslet Lane and Joseph Hobson's Amphitheatre at the corner of King Charles Croft and Lands Lane was followed by 'a meeting of influential gentlemen'. The upshot was the formation of a company with a capital of £50,000 to build a theatre worthy of the town and of 'the support of the very best people'.

£50,000 to build a theatre worthy of the town and of 'the support of the very best people'.

The house in Lyddon Terrace, now part of Leeds University campus, where George Corson lodged as a young architect. Apart from the Grand Theatre, he also designed many other magnificent buildings in Leeds prior to his retirement in 1901. (Leodis Collection/Leeds Library and Information Services)

The directors were members of well known and, for the most part, wealthy families. None of them had previously been involved in the theatre business but they all shared a deep commitment to do their best for Leeds. The Board was West Riding through and through, the professions of the first ten directors showing only too clearly that the theatre was largely financed by 'new' money from the town's burgeoning industry. There were three merchants, a machine maker, a machinist and engineer, an ironmaster, a flax spinner, a maltster, and a card, comb and pin manufacturer. The tenth – and the only member of the professions – was a surgeon. Meetings were reputedly convivial affairs, the directors having their own personal bottles of whisky. With true Yorkshire thrift, they were stored away after each meeting, suitably marked with a line showing the amount that had been consumed!

Whether such conviviality helped is not recorded, but certainly good progress was now made and by May 1877 acquisition had been completed of an ideal three-quarters of an acre site at New Briggate. The design of the building was entrusted to the architect George Corson, first president of the Leeds Architectural Society, who may well have found the project daunting. It has been well said that a successful theatre needs to 'combine the technological complexity of a woollen mill with the focused social activity of a cathedral, and must carry the dying breath of a match-girl to the back bench of the gods'. Corson rose to the challenge and embarked on a tour of the major theatres and opera houses of Europe, noting their individual strengths and collective failings. He returned to the drafting table with the knowledge to complete a masterpiece, but took the additional precaution of engaging his former principal assistant to help with the project. James Robertson Watson had acquired a reputation for designing quality theatres using innovative and dynamic ideas, his obituary referring to his later involvement with York's Theatre Royal, which externally has some marked similarities to the Grand.

The façade of the Grand, full of flamboyant detail with turrets, pillars and a fine rose window. Photographed in June 1936. (Leodis Collection/Leeds Library and Information Services)

'A successful theatre needs to combine the technological complexity of a woollen mill with the focused social activity of a cathedral, and must carry the dying breath of a match-girl to the back bench of the gods'

Building work took thirteen months to complete at a cost of £62,000, the relatively low figure being due to the fact that a trade depression was in full sway. The style adopted was an intriguing mix of Romanesque and Victorian Gothic based on the transitional period of church architecture. Reflecting the high-minded aspirations of the directors, its 170ft long facade included some wonderfully flamboyant decoration such as turrets, pillars and stained glass, the whole surmounted by a splendid rose window. In a far-sighted move to maximise future income, the overall scheme also embraced six shops, Assembly Rooms, a Supper Room and large cellars for wine merchants and for storage. Ahead of its time, it would today have been described as a cultural and shopping centre. Also foreshadowing trends of more recent times, the heart of the building was from the outset conceived as an opera house rather than just a playhouse with the name 'The Grand Theatre and Opera House' being formally adopted in August 1878.

Elaborate detail on the pediment above the entrance to the Assembly Rooms.

The entrance to the Assembly
Rooms with on its left the shops
that were conceived as an integral
part of the development.
(Leodis Collection/Leeds Library
and Information Services)

INSIDE THE GRAND

The Grand was a major milestone in Victorian theatre building and was later described as 'probably the finest of its size in Britain'. It certainly lived up to its name internally as well as externally. The stage area was on a par with the leading London theatres of the day, with dimensions of 118 feet from cellar floor to the apex of the stage roof, 75 feet from footlights to back wall and 72 feet between the walls.

Seating arrangements in the superb auditorium, with three horseshoe-shaped balconies. Note the Royal Boxes at extreme left and right.

Drawings of Grand Theatre from Sachs (1880)

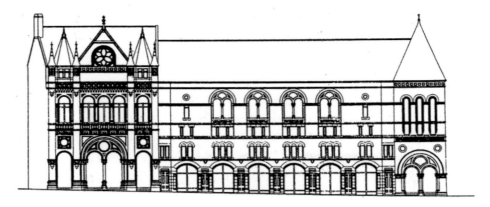

FRONT ELEVATION

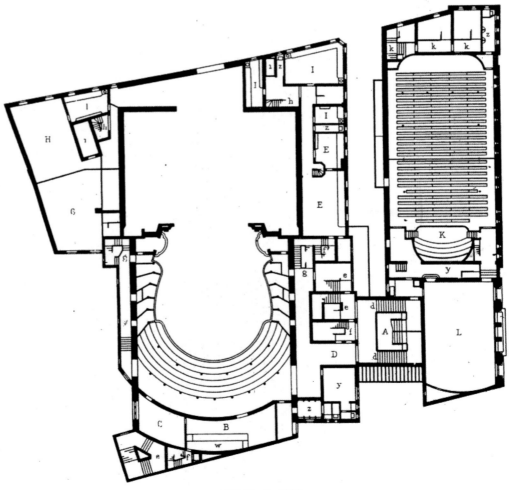

PLAN, II TIER.

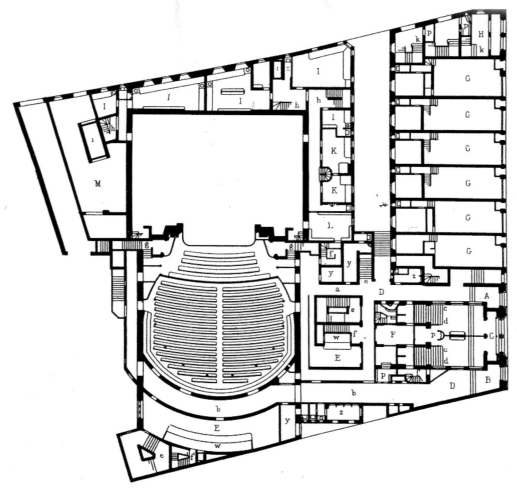

PLAN, AREA.

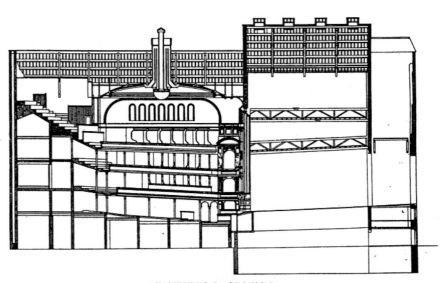

LONGITUDINAL SECTION.

The stunning auditorium comprised three horseshoe-shaped balconies – dress circle, upper circle and gallery – which were decorated with gilded scroll work. It was claimed that careful planning had produced a perfect sightline from almost every seat – a technical achievement unusual in British theatres. The balconies curved downwards and flowed into the elaborately towering proscenium arch, once likened to something 'seemingly halfway between a picture frame and a railway station'! The proscenium wall was joined to the side of the auditorium by clusters of long cylindrical mouldings that resembled organ pipes, the final touch originally being provided by six giant goddesses (later removed and stored, although two have been put back in position as can be seen in the Grand Tour section of this book). Fretted fan vaults extended from the tops of the boxes to a ribbed and domed ceiling, the auditorium as a whole resembling the inside of a densely-decorated egg shell.

It was claimed that careful planning had produced a perfect sightline from almost every seat – a technical achievement unusual in British theatres.

The fan vaults extending from the tops of the boxes to the ceiling. Separating the boxes from the towering proscenium arch are the long cylindrical mouldings that resemble organ pipes. (Yorkshire Post Newspapers – YPN)

The extraordinary ribbed and domed ceiling, sometimes likened to the inside of a richly decorated egg shell. The photograph was taken in September 1982 to mark the installation of a new chandelier. (YPN)

Comfort levels reflected the class-conscious nature of Victorian society, with only the dress circle and boxes being furnished with chairs. All other parts of the house had benches ranging from upholstered in the upper circle to backless and plain wooden in the gallery. Each entrance had its own pay box but a 'transfer staircase' was thoughtfully provided for any patrons who at the last minute decided to better their position by paying more. This could be an expensive exercise at a time when a gallery seat was likely to be sixpence compared with three shillings for the dress circle. Total seating capacity was 2,600, with standing room for another 200, figures that indicate how standards have changed as today the same building will seat 1,450 plus 84 standing. In Victorian times a man was employed to pack as many 'pittites' and 'galleryites' into a row as was humanly possible.

The 1875 destruction of two Leeds theatres may well have influenced the pioneering use of fire-resistant materials and an abundant provision of water hydrants and fire-fighting apparatus. Fireproof staircases using an early form of ferro-concrete connected the many levels and compartments. Exits were especially roomy, undoubtedly as a result of a recent disaster at the Colosseum in Liverpool when people were killed in a panic escape that proved to be a false alarm. Truly innovative was a forerunner of modern sprinkler systems whereby water could be directed through the fifteen miles of pipes that normally fed gas to some 400 gaslights. Until electricity was installed in 1895, gas lit the whole of the Grand other than the stage, which used limelight prepared at the theatre's own plant. Patrons sitting in the wings had the disturbing experience of watching braziers belching out large amounts of smoke as they were fed with powder for coloured lighting effects.

Comfort levels reflected the class-conscious nature of Victorian society, with only the dress circle and boxes being furnished with chairs.

The theatre had the first stage in Britain to be built primarily of iron, bringing with it further benefits of fire prevention. The machinery, also largely of iron, remained in place until its removal in 1979. A height of thirty feet from cellar to stage level came into its own during major productions, the *Yorkshire Post* commenting that it enabled 'a good-sized castle or ship to be sent up from the regions below'. Backstage accommodation was described as 'unequalled', with the dressing rooms being heated by steam pipes. There were two massive frames for the painting of scenery and several miles of speaking tubes for communicating with the various parts of the theatre. The extensive nature of the site meant that there was no difficulty in finding space for an amazing range of facilities that included a carpenters' shop, plumbers' shop, smiths' shop, armoury, wardrobe and sewing rooms, gasfitters' workshop, property workroom and modeling room. There was even a pottery for firing props and utensils. An abundance of traps, bridges and machinery for manipulating transformation schemes completed a remarkable enterprise.

The main staircase at the Grand has always been an eye-catcher, but there were many other 'transfer staircases'. These were provided so that patrons could indulge in what today would be termed a 'late upgrade', moving to better seating with a minimum of inconvenience. (YPN)

OPENING NIGHT

After some last-minute delays, it was finally possible to print a handbill announcing that 'this Magnificent Building will positively open' on November 18th, 1878. Standing or sitting in varying degrees of comfort, the opening-night audience saw for the first time the lush, Italianate auditorium in crimson and gold. When the red velvet curtains lifted, they may well have gasped in surprise as the dropscene was not the usual hackneyed view of Lake Como or the Bay of Naples, but a painting of nearby Kirkstall Abbey completed at a cost of £98 by the artist William Telbin.

Shakespeare's *Much Ado About Nothing* was chosen as the opening performance. There was much speech making and a Glee Party was brought in to sing the National Anthem. Several of the speeches contrasted the Grand Theatre with similar venues in other countries and concluded that 'few of them would compare with this splendid house'. There was trenchant comment about the 'extravagant edifices' of our foreign competitors, often erected by way of municipal powers and public subscription, whereas in Britain it was necessary to rely on commercial success and accordingly 'cut our coat to the size of our cloth'. This, it was claimed, made the excellence of the Grand even more momentous!

'If the stage were to be engulfed in fire, every gentleman would have time to light his cigar comfortably, give his arm to his lady love and saunter pleasantly out of the building!' Wilson Barrett

Masterminding the event was Wilson Barrett, an actor-manager and playwright who at the relatively young age of 32 had been granted a five-year lease of the new theatre at a rental of £1,700 per annum. He had already taken over the Theatre Royal in Hull and rapidly built up a reputation for staging new plays direct from London. Larger than life, he was prone to making speeches from the stage – indeed it was sometimes said that he invented the practice. His opening-night offering was characteristic and touched at length on fire precautions. He colourfully if perhaps a touch optimistically explained: 'If the stage were to be engulfed in fire, every gentleman would have time to light his cigar comfortably, give his arm to his lady love and saunter pleasantly out of the building!'

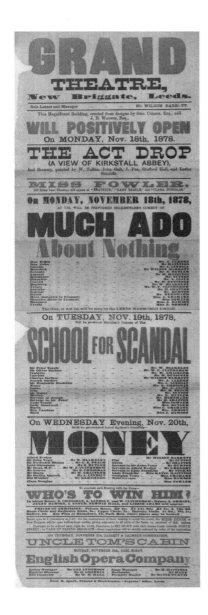

Victorian typography at its finest. The handbill announcing that the Grand Theatre would 'positively open' on November 18th, 1878 with a production of Shakespeare's *Much Ado About Nothing.*

Wilson Barrett, who took a lease of the Grand Theatre when aged only 32. He spearheaded both its opening and early development. (West Yorkshire Archive Service)

A sequel later occurred when a loud explosion shook the auditorium during a performance. Panic was starting to break out among the audience when Barrett suddenly appeared in one of the boxes, jumped onto the parapet and addressed the milling patrons. 'Ladies and gentlemen,' he boomed in his best actor's voice, 'are you English men and women? There is NO need for alarm. A barrel of beer has burst. That is all.' Peace was promptly restored.

In his opening night address, Barrett was clearly aware that theatres were still seen as centres of improper activity by many of the more respectable members of society. He touched on morality and avowed that his aim was to provide plays worthy of being heard and seen – 'plays that would not bring a blush to the youngest girl who might enter the theatre'. A few days later he promised to the then Vicar of Leeds, Dr John Gott, that he would indeed endeavour to give the people of the city 'something to elevate them, something to make them better men and women'. Gott went on to become Bishop of Truro but never forgot the charismatic manager of the Grand. When Barrett's lease of the theatre expired, he received an exquisite Worcester vase inscribed in gold letters: 'From the Bishop of Truro to Wilson Barrett in grateful acknowledgement of a promise nobly kept.'

'My aim is to provide 'plays that would not bring a blush to the youngest girl who might enter the theatre' Wilson Barrett

DOWN THE YEARS

Immediately after the opening night Barrett was busy working on his 'New and Strictly Original Comic Grand Christmas Pantomime' with the grandiose title of *Blue Beard the Grand – or Harlequin the Amorous Ameer*. An opulent and spectacular production with eleven scenes and a cast that included three hundred extras, it ran until the end of February. A surviving daybill hints that traffic problems created by special theatrical events were already evident: 'Carriages to be ordered each night for 10.30. Coachmen to set down with their horses' heads towards North Street; to take up facing Briggate – these regulations will be strictly enforced.'

An event of a very different kind occurred on August 4th, 1879, when the conjuror Dr Lynn opened the Assembly Rooms, alongside but separate from the Grand Theatre itself. Capable of accommodating some 1,200 people, they were in modern jargon multi-functional and designed for such widely differing purposes as bazaars, balls, public meetings, concerts and smaller dramatic performances. The twenty-one feet deep stage was constructed so that it could easily be removed to create more space for dancing. A colourful description appeared in the *Yorkshire Post* the day after the opening: 'The front of the dress circle is elaborately furnished with quilted satin panels and running carton-pierre ornaments, picked out in gold and colours. The rich satin panels give the hall a very warm and cosy appearance, and the room promises to be particularly good in its acoustic properties.'

Back in the main theatre, pantomime became the great provider and set a pattern for a spectacular offering each festive season that was to endure until recent times. There was a period when *Cinderella* came to be regarded as an unlucky pantomime. On one occasion Cinders fell and broke her leg and a later production saw the death of one of the ponies stabled backstage. Way back in 1887 there was another incident when a couple of young men, their spirits uplifted by frequent visits to the circle bar, hurled a large bunch of carrots at Cinders, played by the popular Addie Blanche. They missed their target but Addie's burly fiancé was so incensed that he grabbed the two roisterers by the collar, dragged them down the circle staircase and deposited them in the middle of Briggate.

Another annual event – a show by Leeds Amateur Operatic Society – had its origins as early as 1893 with a performance of *La Fille de Madame Augot* (see page 74). The rest of the year was a mixture of opera, ballet, music hall and plays, with many legendary names treading the boards. In 1885 the running of the theatre was taken over by the directors, with John Hart as manager. He carried out many improvements, including the addition of a canopy over the main entrance in 1894 and the installation of a new stage four years later.

Life for those working at the Grand was then very different to what would be the case today. Long remembered was Harry Tingle, who started work on the opening day as a callboy aged about fourteen. He was still on the staff at the time of his death in 1939, having risen to combine the roles of head fireman and responsibility for the gents' cloakroom. When the full fire round was undertaken it took over four hours to check every room. In the summer months when the theatre was closed (or 'dark') he had to lower the chandelier and clean every piece of it by hand. Harry met his wife Florence Crosland when she was working in the circle bar and they were wed in 1911, but she then promptly had to leave as theatre rules did not allow married couples to work together.

Another name still remembered is Phil May, who came to the Grand as an untrained fifteen-year-old from a back street in the New Wortley district of Leeds. He got a job helping the scene painters, which gave him an opportunity to do watercolours of some of the performers. Phil moved on and after a period in Australia he returned to England as the star cartoonist for *Punch*. It was a post that brought fame and fortune, all of which he drank away.

Life for those working at the Grand was then very different to what would be the case today.

This 1936 photograph gives a good impression of the canopy installed over the main entrance in 1894. It gave patrons some protection from the weather on a wild winter's night. (Leodis Collection/Leeds Library and Information Services)

The two world wars affected the theatre in different ways. In 1914 there was an outbreak of special productions, as instanced by *Sealed Orders*, which was billed as 'a Great Naval and Patriotic Play'. A suitable note was inserted in the programmes: 'It is hoped that the public will, as far as possible, support the theatre during this period of stress. By so doing they will keep in employment a vast number of workers.' The public did just that and it soon became evident that the Grand, together with other theatres, was in for some boom years.

In the months leading up to the outbreak of the second world war in 1939, the Grand took the view that its key role was to provide light relief and mounted a series of farces and musical comedies. Even so, a stern note was struck on one occasion when the Lord Mayor of Leeds took the stage and appealed for volunteers for National Service. He lamented the fact that only 4,000 people out of a population of half a million had enrolled.

The Grand reaped the benefit when wartime theatre restrictions in London forced a number of productions to transfer from the West End to Leeds. It was a great bonus, although this time the programmes conveyed a more serious message: 'In the event of an air raid warning the performance will stop immediately and an announcement will be made from the stage requesting people to leave the theatre in an orderly manner.' There was a postscript that today strikes a comic note but was undoubtedly very real at the time: 'Don't leave your Gas Mask behind on leaving the theatre!'

Despite such fears, it was business as usual with traditional pantomimes such as *Jack and the Beanstalk, The Sleeping Beauty* and *Aladdin* packing in the audiences each season. In the best of theatrical traditions, the Grand never closed.

'Don't leave your Gas Mask behind on leaving the theatre!'

CHANGING TIMES

Peace was celebrated in June 1945 with a week-long victory festival *Youth Marches On!*, produced in association with the *Yorkshire Evening News*. With an enormous cast drawn from eighteen separate youth organisations, it was clearly an ambitious affair with fifteen episodes plus a finale and an epilogue preceding the singing of 'Land of Hope and Glory'. One senses that Baden Powell would have been proud of much of the content, which reflected the spirit of the time: 'Law and Order', 'Youthful Achievement', 'Housewives of the Future' and 'Camp Fire and Community Singing'. The programme stressed that the event was 'Dedicated to the Victorious Peace', but could not hide the fact that times were hard. It regretted that 'rationed space' made it impossible to acknowledge all those whose enthusiastic co-operation had made the production possible. Minimalist adverts on the back give a snapshot of the immediate post-war era by proclaiming that Perry's Powders are 'a boon to British babyhood', Balsham Bros can undertake printing for 'priority and essential services', Shamose leg make-up is supplied by Woodlands chemists, and the Astoria Ballroom is 'the smartest dance rendezvous in Leeds'.

OVER: The finale on the opening night of *Youth Marches On!* – June 4th, 1945. All members of the 500-strong cast took to the stage as a tribute to St. George. Alderman C.V. Walker, the Lord Mayor of Leeds, then read a closing speech, 'The Charge to Youth', which included the words: "The future of this Empire is in the hands of youth and may this youth teach the world what Hitler Youth would have meant to the world and teach them the Hitler type is not their type." It may not have been the greatest speech ever written but it certainly captured the mood of the moment. (Leodis Collection/YPN)

The closing night of *Youth Marches On!* – one week later on June 11th. 'The Charge to Youth' speech is read by Canon A.S. Reeve, the Vicar of Leeds. One of the sketches involved cast members dressing up as well-known personalities famous for great achievements at a young age. On the left, wearing an 18th-century style wig and standing next to the girl with a crown, is Reg Blackshaw from Wortley. Dressed as Mozart, he performed a well-received violin solo. (Leodis Collection/YPN)

The ambitious programme for the June 1945
'Victory' production of *Youth Marches On!*

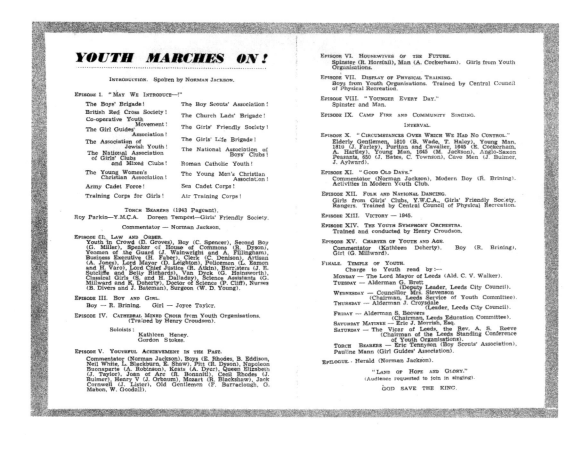

With an enormous cast drawn from eighteen separate youth organisations, it was clearly an ambitious affair with fifteen episodes plus a finale and an epilogue preceding the singing of 'Land of Hope and Glory'.

Patrons at the Grand were able to recover from the rigours and restrictions of wartime with productions that were strong on surprise and innovation. Wilfred Pickles appeared in a straight play *Cure for Love*, proving that he could act as well as host his popular radio show *Have a Go*. Laurence Olivier produced Thornton Wilder's *The Skin of our Teeth*, starring his then wife Vivien Leigh as Sabrina, the embodiment of all pleasure-loving females. Her performance was thought-provokingly described as 'cartooning her sex with an audacity which makes virtue of vice'.

One issue that would not arise today occurred during the 1947 season of Gilbert and Sullivan operas by the D'Oyly Carte company, when a newspaper report noted that the performance was 'dimly discernible through a haze of tobacco smoke'. After an outbreak of coughing by a member of the company, an attendant went round the audience asking them to extinguish their pipes and cigarettes. Smoking in the auditorium was not banned until 1965, when all the ashtrays were removed.

Programme notes from this period are exercises in studied politeness. An example from the late 1940s reads: 'To the Ladies – If your headgear obstructs the view of others, would you kindly remove it. Thank You.' As late as 1954 there was the following notice to patrons: 'In response to many enquiries, the management wish to state that the wearing of evening dress is welcome in the theatre. This, of course, is entirely optional, and those who prefer informal dress can be assured that their patronage is equally appreciated.' John Beaumont, managing director of the Grand for a long run from 1943 through to 1974, later explained: 'I was really thinking of Friday nights when the curtain goes up later and gives people a chance to have a meal and dress first. In pre-war days one could often count the number of people in the circle and stalls who were not in evening dress. On Friday night it was a beautiful sight. I think a well-dressed audience creates a certain atmosphere.'

Royal occasion at the Grand on October 17th, 1958. Conducted by Sir David Webster, general administrator of the Royal Opera House, the Queen meets principals of *Samson*. In the picture are Joan Sutherland and Jon Vickers. (YPN)

This was certainly the case on one of the most glittering occasions in the long history of the Grand Theatre. On October 17th, 1958, the climax of the Leeds Centenary Musical Festival was a performance of Handel's *Samson* in the presence of the Queen and Prince Philip, the Princess Royal and her son Lord Harewood. The sense of occasion in the theatre before the curtain rose was well captured by Marie Hartley and Joan Ingilby in their book *The Wonders of Yorkshire*:

'Each petal of the massed chrysanthemums decorating the royal box lay crisp and fresh, one upon the other. Evening dresses shimmered beneath fur stoles. Diamonds, pearls and medals glittered. Laughter and talk filled the auditorium.'

Helen Shapiro

The Shadows with Cliff Richard

Yet this red-letter day could scarcely disguise the fact that storm clouds were gathering on the horizon. Radio had already threatened the presence of patrons and then came what the theatre's centenary publication succinctly described as 'the deadlier thrust of television, with audiences tending to melt faster than ice cream held in the diminishing number of hot hands in the stalls'.

In 1962 a dearth of summer touring shows of suitable standard led to a startling departure that displeased the more seriously minded patrons. The tables were in a sense turned with a series of musical variety shows featuring stars whose popularity owed much to television. They included Helen Shapiro, The Shadows and Frankie Vaughan, who packed the theatre to the gods with near hysterical devotees, applauding an entertainer who had once lived among them.

'the deadlier thrust of television, with audiences tending to melt faster than ice cream held in the diminishing number of hot hands in the stalls'.

Although the Grand had to close its doors the following summer for want of suitable attractions, the idea took root and in 1964 was developed into a nine-week Television Star Season. A simple but effective idea that made theatrical history, it involved putting on plays featuring well-known TV artists who happened to be 'resting' from their studio commitments. It brought to Leeds the stars from such blockbusters of the small screen as 'Z-Cars' and 'Emergency Ward 10'.

The season kept the box office till ringing and was happily followed early in 1965 by a show that ran for a record-breaking four months. *My Fair Lady* was the biggest and most spectacular production handled at the Grand to that date. Its successful staging was a tribute to the size and facilities of the theatre, as it was the first time since leaving Drury Lane that the London company had been able to bring the whole scenery – with its two 'revolves' – and lighting into action.

The Grand, photographed in August 1966, when *My Fair Lady* was making a return visit following its spectacularly successful four-month run the previous year. Only three years later the theatre was threatened with demolition, a planning application for a replacement office block concluding that the quality of the frontage did not justify preservation. (Leodis Collection)

My Fair Lady paved the way for an even more elaborate production the following year, when Lionel Bart's hit musical *Oliver* came to Leeds for almost seven weeks. Famous as the longest running musical in the history of the British theatre, it boasted a pre-set electronically operated stage and attracted vast audiences.

Appearances in the 1960s by comedians of the stature of Tony Hancock and Harry Secombe, as well as such heavyweight actors as John Gielgud and Alec Guinness, also helped to better the financial picture. Yet the theatrical world is notoriously fickle and it was perhaps inevitable that sooner or later a disaster would occur. It came in 1968 with the 'Leeds Festival of Drama', a twelve-week series of plays put on at short notice to avoid opening the historic portals of the Grand to the demeaning exercise of Bingo. On one night the audience numbered little more than a score and the venture as a whole lost the then considerable sum of some £15,000.

Only a few months later John Beaumont sounded a stark warning. A 'serious state of affairs' meant that the curtain could be about to fall for good, the problem of diminishing audiences being accentuated by the unwillingness of players to leave the south, where they were within easy reach of TV contacts and contracts. Hitherto, rents from the property around the theatre had kept it going but now these were being absorbed in the losses.

John Beaumont commented: 'The Grand is no ordinary theatre. It is a building of historic interest. Such a theatre is an asset to a city and draws people into it from far and near. A city of this size without a theatre is a city without a soul.' He nevertheless indicated that unless Leeds Corporation was prepared to take over the Grand 'lock stock and barrel' then planning permission would have to be sought to redevelop the site.

Tony Hancock

John Gielgud

Plans to demolish Leeds Grand Theatre

22 MAR 1969

1487S

Yorkshire Post Reporter

PLANS to pull down the Grand Theatre, Leeds, built in 1878, and officially classed as a protected building of architectural and historical interest, are to be discussed by a policy-making sub-committee of Leeds City Council.

This move follows a surprise planning application made in Leeds yesterday for the demolition of the theatre, together with the Plaza Cinema and shops

Partners, a Leeds firm of chartered accountants, presented the plans to yesterday's committee.

A memorandum accompanying the formal appli-

depend on what these proposals are, if any are made."

On the other hand, Col. G. H. Kitson, chairman of the theatre's Board, told me

AN ARTIST'S IMPRESSION of the redeveloped site of the Grand Theatre, Leeds. The buildings adjoining The Headrow, including the Odeon, are not involved.

Stark headline in the *Yorkshire Post* of March 22nd, 1969, with accompanying drawing showing the 'skyscraper' office blocks that would have replaced the Grand Theatre.

The predictable result was an outcry based more on sentiment than harsh economics. The singer and impresario John Hanson echoed the views of many: 'It is one of the loveliest of theatres. It is quite unique – its interior, its block of dressing rooms, its large stage. In a city the size of Leeds the Council should make it its business to keep the theatre open. It would be quite a tragedy if it closed. You cannot replace old theatres. The new ones never have the atmosphere, the warmth, that help to give the audience that feeling of a night out.'

They were fine words but were probably scarcely considered when in March 1969 a policy-making sub-committee of Leeds City Council discussed plans for what today would seem barely conceivable – a replacement 22-storey office block alongside another of 20 floors and extensive shopping facilities. The planning application dismissively commented that the Grand was too small to carry economically any spectacular or ambitious production and declared that externally the true merit and quality of the Briggate frontage did not justify preservation. The future looked bleak.

A 'serious state of affairs' meant that the curtain could be about to fall for good.

A NEW ERA

Happily the planning application to demolish and redevelop was turned down, a prime reason being that in 1963 the theatre had become a Grade II 'listed' building of special architectural or historic interest. This meant that demolition would have required the consent of the Ministry of Housing and Local Government and there may well have been doubts as to whether this would be obtained. Nevertheless, there remained great anxiety until the glad tidings were received in mid-December 1969 that Leeds City Council was to take a lease for a minimum of seven years and arrange for a Trust to operate the theatre. The Grand had been saved.

A promise was given that it would remain 'a live theatre, providing the finest touring productions in opera, ballet and drama for the people of Leeds and the West Riding'. With John Beaumont continuing as managing director, this promise was quickly put into effect and a varied bill advertised that contained something for everybody. The new era opened with *Lady Frederick*, the first play written by the prolific Somerset Maugham, which starred Margaret Lockwood and Tony Britton. The next production saw Doncaster-born Diana Rigg perform a much-publicised nude scene with what was described as 'exquisite taste' in Ronald Millar's new play *Abelard and Heloise*. There was plenty of laughter from such seasoned performers as Brian Rix and Alastair Sim, and then at the end of 1970 came a six-week run of the rock musical *Hair* complete with bells, beads, incense and flowers.

The results were decidedly encouraging with a net profit of more than £8,000 being made in the first twelve months of the new regime. It was in this happier situation that John Beaumont retired and was succeeded by Warren Smith, who at the young age of twenty-five came to the Grand in 1971 as house manager. He soon became the theatre's general manager and happily is still at the helm, remarkably being only the fifth person to hold the post in the Grand's entire 128-year history. He still recalls his first impressions: 'I had seen nothing like it before. Inside it was all dark maroon paint looking as though it had not been touched for umpteen years. It was an old-fashioned interior with a dress circle bar like a 1930s liner.'

Saving the Grand

My family had 'regular seats' at the Grand. One evening we learnt from the attendants that their jobs were to terminate in a month as the theatre was to close, be pulled down, and an office block to be built on the site.

Appalled, I was determined to stop this going forward. With the support of my father who contacted Equity, I started to get people to write to Leeds City Council objecting to the plan. When I had several hundred letters supporting me I took the whole thing to John Hepper at the Civic Trust. He took up the cause and put it before the Council. The result was a stop on the proposed demolition, a grant for renovation and ultimately help to Opera North to become based at Leeds Grand.

Ann Smith

A £1 million restoration began in the same year and gave the theatre the latest type of lighting equipment and an extended orchestra pit as well as modern scenery and effects. A massive and long overdue repainting and refurnishing of the auditorium was also put in hand. These developments paved the way for more good news in July 1973, when Leeds City Council bought the Grand and its adjoining property from Howard & Wyndham, the London-based theatre chain, who through a share deal had become the effective owners the previous year. The price paid was some £355,000.

Warren Smith – a recent photograph taken in the auditorium. When he came to the Grand in 1971 he found an old-fashioned theatre that looked as if it had 'not been touched for umpteen years'.

Much needed improvements to the theatre were put in hand in 1971 and included the latest type of stage and house lighting, controlled from a computer consol that in those days was far from tiny. Jeff Riley, an electrician, is seen demonstrating it to visitors Kath Wardle and her daughter Chrissie, aged six, on a 'Grand Open Day'. (YPN)

One of Warren Smith's first successes was to instigate a Festival of Youth Theatre with over 700 schoolchildren from thirty schools presenting such diverse entertainment as Shakespeare, the story of the Great Plague, brass band music and Gilbert & Sullivan. Another new trend was the presentation of rock shows, the volume of sound from the likes of Showaddywaddy and the Bay City Rollers being so great that experts were called in to check if the theatre's plaster ceiling could withstand sound waves at this level. Happily the answer was in the affirmative, paving the way for a whole series of pop concerts that brought a new level of exuberance to the Grand. Appearances by international stars such as Billy Connolly and Gene Pitney, as well as British entertainers ranging from Ken Dodd to Bruce Forsyth, stressed that the theatre was now also a Variety Hall. At the other end of the scale, members of the audience commented favourably on the realism of a macabre hanging scene in Hermiston, a new work by Scottish Opera, unaware that the actor strung up on stage had actually passed out!

Despite such incidents, matters were now definitely on the up as shown by a record-breaking twelve months ending in April 1976 when no less than 326,000 patrons watched 400 different performances. A major innovation in this period was that the finals of the internationally acclaimed Leeds International Pianoforte Competition were for the first time held at the Grand. A special screen was made to prevent sounds being lost in the cavernous background of the stage, although this did not prevent Radu Lupu, winner of the 1969 contest, denouncing the choice of venue: 'The Grand is acoustically terrible!' Such damning criticism was ultimately ineffective, as the finals were televised and brought the splendours of the Grand to a whole new audience. The theatre had come a long way in its first hundred years.

The special exhibition held at the Grand in September 1978 on the occasion of its centenary. Looking round are, left to right: Councillor Peter Sparling; Mrs Booth, the Lady Mayoress of Leeds; Warren Smith, the theatre's manager; Councillor Booth, the Lord Mayor; and T M Collinson, the city's chief archivist. (YPN)

THE GRAND

Theatre & Opera House Leeds

✳ 1878~1978 ✳

STAR PERFORMERS

(AN ALPHABETICAL SELECTION)

Julie Andrews

Came to the Grand in 1954 as an appealing teenager in her first play, *Mountain of Fire*. The play was forgettable but Julie was memorable. The *Evening Post* theatre critic, John Bolton, proclaimed: 'The youngest sure claimant for stardom I have met recently. Besides an immense natural talent, she has a thoroughly professional mind and a willingness to work and learn.'

Stanley Baxter

Regularly appeared in pantomime at the Grand – and especially in *Mother Goose*. The occasion when he appeared to have a goose on his head was long remembered.

Bay City Rollers

Created pandemonium that is still remembered. By mid-afternoon there were police horses down the street and two barriers on Briggate to hold back the crowds. Kids with only one ticket between them were tying themselves together with tartan scarves. After the show the teenybop band was smuggled out through a secret back door in the basement and into a truck in Vicar Lane.

Sarah Bernhardt

The most famous French actress of her day made her first visit to Leeds in July 1881 for *La Dame Aux Camelias*. According to one critic, audiences were more interested in what they saw than what they heard.

Cicely Courtneidge

Had her first stage part at the Grand in the early 1900s, playing Peaseblossom in her father's production of *A Midsummer Night's Dream*.

'An Evening with Dickie Bird'

I shall never forget performing at the Grand Theatre, Leeds. It is a wonderful memory I shall always treasure.

That evening the theatre was packed to capacity – not a seat anywhere. It was a sell out. The manager told me he could have filled the theatre many times if he had had a larger building. He said to me, 'Dickie – you have sold me more seats than we sold for Shirley Bassey. When he said that it meant so much to me and made my evening. I was so proud to be part of a great evening enjoyed by everyone.

It was a tremendous honour for me to be invited to perform at this wonderful Victorian theatre. It is steeped in history, the home of legends, and here I was – a test cricket umpire – performing in this beautiful theatre where all the great artists throughout the world have performed. As I looked round I felt so very humble.

We should all be so very proud of the Grand Theatre, right through the country, the world and of course here in Yorkshire. When I played for Yorkshire County Cricket Club, all the players liked to come to the theatre to see the shows.

Well done to everybody concerned and to all who have put all their efforts into this great Victorian theatre.

It was a tremendous honour for me to be invited to perform at this wonderful Victorian theatre.

Les Dawson and Ronnie Hilton

Regularly appeared in pantomime at the Grand. Commenting on his popular panto-partnership with Ronnie Hilton, Les once said: 'Tell my fans that I consider it part of my charity work. I don't like to see old men hanging about in the streets.' Ronnie quipped that working in Leeds, where he could be at home and near his beloved football team, made up for working with Dawson!

Ken Dodd

Infamous for his habit of overrunning and turning his shows into four-hour marathons. Warren Smith, manager at the Grand, effectively thwarted this habit:

'Ken is brilliant but two-and-a-half-hours of anyone is enough, so when he comes off you have to grab his drum before he goes back on for yet another encore.'

Geraint Evans

Stormed off the stage when a new computerised lighting system was introduced in 1971. He thought the chief electrician, sitting with headphones on, was recording his singing – and it was quite a task to convince him otherwise!

Margot Fonteyn

Gave a 'faultless performance' in November 1972, dancing with Attilio Labis the English premiere of the *Romeo and Juliet* pas de deux, choreographed by George Skibine. The house applauded its head off, hurling flowers onto the stage with one bunch of very wet roses hitting a member of the orchestra a nasty wet smack in the nape of the neck. On another occasion, Dame Margot gave a captivating performance as the principal ballerina in Tchaikovsky's *Swan Lake*, although unfortunately she had broken her big toe and only came on stage for ten minutes.

A truly special theatre

I have played many UK concert tours over the past thirty years and have always looked forward to the Leeds Grand Theatre date. I can honestly say that every time I have played there the atmosphere and the reaction of the packed houses has been terrific. It's as if you can reach out and touch the audience. The atmosphere and warmth of the audience is of course something to do with the people attending but I'm sure this special venue really contributes to a warm and memorable occasion.

As a performer on the stage of the Grand you can feel I think the echoes of journeys of the past. Performers that came to communicate over many years, the laughter, tears and applause of past and present generations of theatre goers, their soul prints still present.

Stories told and the music played seem embedded in the very fabric of the Grand – a truly special theatre.

David Essex

George Formby

Brought pre-war glamour back to the Grand when he starred in the 1946 pantomime *Dick Whittington*. One reviewer noted that he was everything his admirers expected of him – good-humoured, sprightly and playing his famous ukelele as well.

Barry Humphries (Dame Edna)

Caused a stir by going straight from the theatre to a local art gallery still in full 'Dame Edna' costume. People there were suspicious, especially when he/she didn't buy any art!

Henry Irving

The first actor to receive a knighthood, Irving appeared at the Grand over a period of almost a quarter of a century from 1880 to 1904. A year later he died in the foyer of Bradford's Midland Hotel after famously delivering the last words in Tennyson's play *Becket*: 'Into Thy hands, O Lord, into Thy hands.'

Elton John

Much younger when he came to Leeds, he had the audience in the palm of his hand and surprised all present by leaping off the stage and strolling casually along the narrow rail of the orchestra pit. He had arrived with two 'heavies', big burly men who stood either side of his dressing room door.

Gordon Kaye

The 'Allo 'Allo actor once walked out of a production after the first act, forgetting there was still one more to go.

Felicity Kendal

Created a challenge in 1972 when she appeared in John Ford's *Tis Pity She's a Whore*, the part requiring her to display all stages of pregnancy. The difficulty was that she was actually pregnant at the time, so her real condition had to be hidden at the beginning of the play.

Lily Langtry

The daughter of the Dean of Jersey was more renowned for her stunning looks and social position than her acting ability. Came to Leeds for the first time in June 1881 in *She Stoops to Conquer*.

Beatrice Lilly (Lady Peel)

During the second world war she learnt on the morning of her stage performance that her son had been killed in action. She carried on calmly with her act, the audience unaware of her sadness until later.

Marie Lloyd

The greatest name in music hall came to the Grand for several successive weeks in April 1898.

Jessie Matthews

Featured in a noted non-event. Due to open in May 1939 in a play *I Can Take It*, she was unable to go on stage as a result of laryngitis. Her understudy had just undergone an operation, so another actress was summoned on stage – and duly fainted! Theatregoers were sent home.

Morecambe and Wise

Although seen as inseparable, they were chalk and cheese and never occupied a dressing room together. They had a public persona but like all double acts they lived their own lives.

Robert Morley

Kicked up a great fuss when he found that all there was in his dressing room was a bus seat. It was one of a job lot acquired from the corporation so that actors had something to sit on in the wings.

Ivor Novello

Brought *The Dancing Years* to the Grand during the second world war. At least one performance was marked by the sounding of air raid sirens.

Laurence Olivier

During rehearsals he was found at the top of a ladder. On being asked what he was doing up there, it was explained that he was fixing the rain machine. In one of the scenes the rain had to come onto the window at a specific angle and Olivier would not allow anyone else to undertake this work.

Peter O'Toole

Takings were what was then a record £36,000 when O'Toole brought his controversial Old Vic production of *Macbeth* to the Grand for one week in October 1980. It had been universally condemned by London critics, arguably proving once again that all publicity is good publicity. During the visit O'Toole went back to many of his old haunts in Leeds, recalling the four years he spent on the former *Yorkshire Evening News* as darkroom boy.

Anna Pavlova

The Russian ballerina had achieved such worldwide fame in 1912 that the normally unstoppable run of post-Christmas pantomime was interrupted to enable her to appear with the Imperial Ballet. The performances were so successful that she returned twice in the same year.

Cliff Richard

Arriving at the theatre several hours before his evening's performance, he surprised everyone by putting a stool in the middle of the stage at 2pm and asking everyone to leave. He then sat there for the next three hours, 'absorbing the auditorium' because he thought it was so beautiful and playing his guitar.

Danny la Rue

Made his first visit to the Grand for the 1962-63 pantomime *Cinderella*, dressed in the gown Jayne Mansfield wore in the film *Too Hot to Handle*.

Showaddywaddy

Trouble seemed to be brewing when a number of 'teddy boys' and their partners wanted to jive and rock-'n'-roll in the orchestra pit. The front-of-house management wanted to stop it. Dave Bartram, the lead singer, proclaimed that rock-'n'-roll was made for dancing – and so they should dance. A big cheer and rousing applause from the audience resounded round the theatre. They kept on dancing and there was no trouble.

Tommy Steele

Twenty years after singing the blues on the TV programme Six Five Special, he brought his Tommy Steele Anniversary Show to the Grand and drew capacity audiences twice nightly.

Ellen Terry

First appeared at the Grand in autumn 1880, playing Beatrice in *Much Ado About Nothing*. Famed as Henry Irving's leading lady, the two being widely regarded as one of the greatest partnerships of all time.

Dame Sybil Thorndike

The life-long partnership of Dame Sybil and Lewis Casson was forged at the Grand. She was appearing with Casson in Bernard Shaw's *Widowers' Houses*. One day they sneaked out of the stage door and headed for a jewellers' in Briggate where they chose an engagement ring. They married a few months later and became one of the most distinguished of theatrical couples. Dame Sybil once said of the Grand: 'There's a quickness of response here that you don't get anywhere else, and a warmth of appreciation. You feel it coming out to you as the play goes on.'

Fanny Waterman

The renowned Leeds classical pianist and her late husband Geoffrey de Keyser were great fans of Ken Dodd (see above). At one of his performances Dr de Keyser commented, 'Hasn't Ken got terrible varicose veins?' 'No,' he was told, 'they're the tag lines to all his jokes, which he writes on his hands in biro!'

Timothy West

The following extract relates to the time when I was in charge at the Old Vic, and the company came to Leeds with the notorious Peter O'Toole Macbeth, *in repertoire with* The Merchant of Venice, *in which I was playing Shylock.*

One night in Leeds, I had only just made it. Because of a meeting of our Heads of Department first thing in the morning, I had let the afternoon's rehearsal run on half an hour longer than I should have done, and then, thanks to a traffic jam, missed my train at King's Cross. The next one got me in to Leeds only ten minutes before the curtain went up, but luckily, not being in the first of two scenes, I was on stage just in time. When I made my last exit after the trial scene I heaved a sigh of relief, and there being a little while before I was needed for the curtain call, I went along to the backstage bar (not many theatres have this old-fashioned facility; the Leeds Grand is one of the very few left) and asked for a whisky. I had no money on me, being in costume, so I asked the lady behind the bar if she would put it on a slate.

She looked at me in my eighteenth-century gaberdine coat and breeches, my yarmulke, curls and false nose, and asked dubiously, 'Are you in the play, love?'

(Reprinted from A Moment Towards the End of the Play *by Timothy West)*

Susannah York, photographed at the Grand in November 1963 when she was appearing in a new play *Wings of the Dove*. Adapted from Henry James' novel, the production later moved to the West End. (Leodis Collection/West Yorkshire Archive)

OTHER FAMOUS NAMES THAT HAVE APPEARED DOWN THE YEARS INCLUDE:

Jack Buchanan	**Alec Guinness**	**Margaret Lockwood**
Jasper Carrott	**Rex Harrison**	**Ralph Richardson**
Sean Connery	**Frankie Howerd**	**Tommy Trinder**
Billy Connolly	**Eddie Izzard**	**Peter Ustinov**
Bruce Forsyth	**Peter Kay**	**Frankie Vaughan**
Joyce Grenfell	**Gertrude Lawrence**	**Susannah York**

Many found the new 1990 production of Verdi's *Jerusalem* difficult to understand, but it nevertheless epitomised Opera North's determination to avoid always doing the obvious. (Hanson/ON)

OPERA TO THE FORE

As the Grand Theatre headed towards its centenary, a milestone occurred for serious music lovers when English National Opera put on the entire four-part production of Wagner's epic masterpiece *The Ring of the Nibelungs*. The first provincial performance in English for four decades, it echoed a production at the Grand back in 1913 when Thomas Beecham and the Denhof Opera Company had presented the complete cycle with performances stretching over an entire week. Much more recently in 1965 there had been the staging of another Wagnerian feast, *The Valkyrie*, when the work's length of almost six hours was punctuated by two intervals. The second was close on an hour long, imparting a Glyndebourne atmosphere as champagne corks popped and cold collations were consumed to the accompaniment of excited chatter.

The involvement of English National Opera was far more significant than was immediately obvious. Behind the scenes, discussions were already taking place that were to usher in the greatest single change in the Grand's long and distinguished history. In November 1977 it was announced that the Grand Theatre and Opera House was truly to reflect the second part of its title and be the home of a new opera company. What soon became known as Opera North was an imaginative extension of English National Opera, whereby a section of the London Coliseum Company moved to Leeds and also took on the majority of the touring commitments. Although sharing some of the London company's facilities until it became fully independent in 1981, Opera North had from the outset its own principal singers, permanent orchestra and chorus, as well as its own conductors, music staff and producers. Supported by the Arts Council, it was the first full-time opera company to be formed in England for more than thirty years.

Lord Harewood, managing director of English National Opera, echoed the spirit of optimism and innovation when he referred to the new venture as 'the best musical opportunity in this country since the war'. Considering the Grand Theatre to be 'the perfect home for an opera company bent on making Yorkshire a musical power-house', he went on to explain that Opera North would be a new kind of conception with productions specifically designed for the Leeds stage. High on the list of priorities were symphony concerts by the orchestra and recitals by artistes, together with concerts both experimental and specially geared to children.

'the best musical opportunity in this country since the war'.

David Lloyd-Jones, the first musical director of Opera North. One critic referred to 'a sturdy figure bringing vibrancy to every opera'.

It was Lord Harewood who gave the top creative job of musical director to David Lloyd-Jones, hitherto assistant musical director of English National Opera. He had the unenviable task of setting up the company in between conducting at the Coliseum. Hundreds of musicians were auditioned, an orchestra and chorus formed, and administrative, production and technical staff recruited. The company burst into life and hit the ground running with the opening performance of Saint-Saen's *Samson and Delilah* on November 15th, 1978, a date that happily coincided with the Grand Theatre's centenary. It was not an obvious choice but not doing the obvious was to become a trademark of the company down the years. Moreover, the critics were enthusiastic, hailing the new company as 'a reality greater than the promise' and commenting that 'a star was born in Leeds'. *Samson and Delilah* had the virtue of being a big opera for the chorus, under its first chorus master John Pryce-Jones, and for the English Northern Philharmonia (later known as the Orchestra of Opera North) led from the start by David Greed and conducted by Lloyd-Jones.

Samson and Delilah, the opening production of Opera North with John Rawnsley as the High Priest, Gilbert Py as Samson and Katherine Pring as Delilah. It was received with great euphoria. (Forbes Henderson/Opera North - ON)

A stunning early production in March 1979 was Benjamin Britten's *Peter Grimes*, one of several that swiftly established Opera North's reputation and swelled box office receipts. (Tony Cryer/ON)

The opening performance was followed by what was described as 'a bold, almost revolutionary experiment' when viewed in the context of the Grand's annual production cycle. The pantomime season was shortened to make way for three operas calculated to capture the spirit of family enjoyment. Offenbach's *Orpheus in the Underworld*, with its heady adventures and abundant comedy, preceded two fairy tales full of magic and glorious improbability – Humperdinck's *Hansel and Gretel* and Mozart's *The Magic Flute*. Then came *Die Fledermaus* followed immediately by *Peter Grimes*.

David Denton, music critic of the *Yorkshire Post*, shared the elation of these early productions: 'Every moment of Britten's *Peter Grimes*, staged a few months into the company's life, is burned into my memory, the chorus armed with cudgels coming to the very edge of the stage to scream the name of Grimes, and you were face to face with a mob hunting you. Those who taped the performance – the BBC being present in those early years – are still in no doubt that in this opera Lloyd-Jones was in a class of his own.'

A pattern gradually emerged whereby Opera North toured for much of the year to other theatres in such cities as Hull, Sheffield, Nottingham, Manchester and Newcastle. It nevertheless occupied the stage and auditorium of the Grand for some twenty-one weeks each year for stage rehearsals and performances. Northern Ballet Theatre (see page 76), also based in Leeds, premiered its productions over a further four weeks with the remainder of the year being devoted to a mixed programme based on a policy of 'something for everyone' – predominantly musicals with some plays, children's shows and concerts. Pantomimes were taken out of the loop, partly because of Opera North's residency at that time of year but also due to the new West Yorkshire Playhouse assuming responsibility for staging the city's major Christmas production. In 1998/99, the best year for some time, the Grand presented 316 performances – including 51 by Opera North – that drew a total attendance of 273,401. A three-week run of *Jesus Christ Superstar* playing to packed houses, coupled with a successful *Joseph and the Amazing Technicolor Dreamcoat*, helped to create an operating surplus of £232,000 – a major turnaround from a deficit of £81,000 only two years earlier.

In 1998/99, the best year for some time, the Grand presented 316 performances – including 51 by Opera North – that drew a total attendance of 273,401.

Schoolchildren and teaching staff attending an Opera North 'Open Day' – June 12th, 1985. (YPN)

A glittering production of *Joseph and the Amazing Techicolor Dreamcoat* helped in the revival of the Grand's fortunes as the twentieth century drew to a close.

Opera North at Leeds Grand, evocatively portrayed in a painting by Selina Thorp. The production is Verdi's *Don Carlos*

Opera North proved to be a visionary partnership, based on a strong belief that opera should be unashamedly egalitarian in its appeal. It soon established itself as one of the leading arts organisations in the country with a reputation as one of the most imaginative opera companies in Europe. Versatility became a keynote, with the ability to programme in a single season both Verdi's early grand opera Jerusalem and Jerome Kern's forerunner of the modern musical *Show Boat*. This was in 1989/90, when Jerusalem was such a controversial production that many of those intimately involved in bringing it to the stage confessed they found it totally mystifying!

Opera North has in fact thrived on controversy, its work affirming that some of the most adventurous and cutting-edge theatre is now to be found in the opera house. Landmark productions have included such off-the-wall choices as Prokofiev's madcap comic opera *The Love for Three Oranges*, described by its director Richard Jones as 'a bit like being thrown through a vortex – the most fantastical and extraordinary thing you've ever seen'. Staging works like Borodin's *Prince Igor*, with its reputation for being unperformable, has similarly posed no terrors. The company has also coped with the occasional disaster, as in 1983/84 when the weight of the set for the new *Die Fledermaus* was such that it disappeared through the stage floor!

The 1999 staging of *La Traviata* starred Tom Randle as Alfredo and Janis Kelly as Violetta. Her performance was described as 'outstanding' and 'perhaps first among equals'.
(Alistair Muir/ON)

The outrageously funny version of Prokoviev's *The Love for Three Oranges*, first performed in 1988 and seen here in its 1993 revival. (Hanson/ON)

Leeds audiences took it all in their stride and displayed their total enjoyment, helped by pride in having their own resident company. They looked forward to seeing such singers as the tenor Robert Ferguson, baritone John Rawnsley and the young sopranos Kate Flowers and Fiona Kim. Opera-goers have their own special memories. One cites the 1984 performance of *Tosca* and the Te Deum at the end of Act I as 'one of those spine-tingling, hair-standing-up-at-the-back-of-the-neck moments'. Another recalls the staging of Verdi's *La Traviata*, 'brilliantly performed' by Janis Kelly. From the outset, Opera North attracted patronage from a wide geographical area with many Lancashire devotees regularly driving across the Pennines in convoy. One relates how she was so keen to see productions that she moved to Leeds in 1983. When she applied for a post as a solicitor she was told at interview: 'I think your real reason for wanting this job is because Opera North perform in Leeds and not the job itself.' She still got the post!

It was a great blow to many when David Lloyd-Jones' tenure as musical director came to an end, although there is little doubt that his successor, a young and ebullient Paul Daniel, took Opera North to even greater heights. His presentation of Berg's *Wozzeck*, described as 'probably the most realistic and disturbing we shall ever see', was followed by a new production of Britten's *Gloriana* that was hailed as the company's greatest achievement.

By the time of its silver jubilee in 2003, those associated with Opera North were able to look forward with confidence. Its patron, the Duke of Kent, described the company as 'a jewel in the nation's artistic crown' and 'a major influence in the development of the cultural scene of the North of England'. These views were echoed by the then Minister of State for the Arts, Estelle Morris, who praised the innovative programming of 'a true champion of musical theatre'. There was also praise from Lord Harewood, one of it most fervent supporters: 'Opera goers within reach, and some from further afield, have a broader operatic perspective now than twenty-five years ago. That's something, maybe not to induce pride, but at least pleasure.'

Opera North has never been afraid of controversy. Demonstrators gathered outside the theatre on October 3rd, 1990 during the premiere of *The Threepenny Opera* – featuring the song 'Mac the knife'. They maintained that extra scenes had been added, glorifying sexual violence against women, and demanded that they be cut. (YPN)

THE AUDITORIUM ... FRIENDLY, WARM, FRIGHTENING

Josephine Barstow

My memories of the Grand go back a long way. It features in the frequent visits I made to the city as a child. The black city where my father was born and where my mother taught in the school opposite front-of-house. She had to leave that job because I, the first child, was on the way. In her day there was no alternative. I don't think she ever quite forgave me. I remember the excitement of visits to the pantomime; did they sow the seeds of the future?

Later there are memories of my husband relating his memories of 'get ins' by horse and cart! – can that be right? – attended by the fear of losing everything in an unscheduled and precipitous descent of the steep hill down to Vicar Lane. He remembered the digs in Briggate opposite the theatre and being kept awake by trams rattling by under the window.

Then my own memories as a performer begin. Mostly relatively recently in productions for lovely Opera North. One always feels a huge affection for theatres in which one has so often performed. One spends so much time lost inside for rehearsals, oblivious to the doings of the outside world, the weather, time of day, everything.

In the case of the Grand these memories are tinged with exasperation. It wasn't always pleasant locked in there. The current renovations are much needed. The dressing room which so often became a second home did not always smell sweet, in defiance of all the efforts of its occupants! All that was relieved by the faithful, wonderful presence of Friede, one of the Grand's most precious assets. Ever ready with cup of tea, sympathetic ear, unfailing support, wizardry with button and zip and many a laugh, not to mention expert dog minding! – Vital.

And the auditorium from the stage, beautiful and near enough to have proper contact with the audience, a huge relief after barns abroad. Friendly, warm, frightening.

And the stage itself: place of work, of shared effort, of disappointment, of weariness and occasional moments of inspiration shared and understood.

Josephine Barstow as Queen Elizabeth I in the 2001/02 version of *Gloriana*, the opera associated with the company's finest achievements. (Stephen Vaughan/ON)

'THE AMATEURS'

A very different kind of opera with its own loyal band of followers has appeared on the stage of the Grand for well over a hundred years. Leeds Amateur Operatic and Dramatic Society – always known in the nicest sense of the term as 'The Amateurs' – was founded in 1890 at a meeting believed to have taken place at the Fenton Hotel in Woodhouse Lane. Unable to afford the cost of appearing at a major theatre, it gave its first production, *HMS Pinafore*, at the Leeds Rifles Barracks in Carlton Hill. It cost £102 but resulted in a healthy profit with donations of £62 to charities.

Handbill announcing the Society's first production at the Grand in 1893.

Problems in staging productions at The Coliseum in Cookridge Street resulted in a decision to perform Lecocq's comic opera *La Fille de Madame Angot* at the Grand during Easter week of 1893. A surviving handbill proclaimed that 'no expense has been spared to make the production as complete as possible and thoroughly worthy of the magnificent theatre where it will take place'. It listed twenty ladies and gentlemen who were to take part together with a full chorus of sixty performers and a 'specially augmented band'. Costumes had been designed by Karl and made by Messrs L and H Nathan, Court Costumiers, Coventry Street, London.

It must all have been a great success as the 'Leeds Amateurs' never looked back. With the exception of the two World Wars and the recent closure for refurbishment, they have appeared every year at the Grand without a break. Their performance of *Ragtime* in March 2007 will be the one-hundredth production that the company has staged at the theatre.

The stage of the Grand is seen at its best in this chorus scene during the 2001 production of *My Fair Lady*.

The following year *Carousel* was performed to equally good effect.

Front cover of the programme for the 1919 presentation of *Merrie England*.

Swan Lake with Jonathan Byrne Olivier and Keiko Amemori. (Brian Slater)

DANCING YEARS

Another company that has become intimately associated with the Grand is the Northern Ballet Theatre, founded in 1969 as the Northern Dance Theatre by Canadian-born Laverne Meyer. With just eleven dancers, it survived its early years through determination, hard work and inventiveness. By 1987 the size of the company had more than doubled to twenty-eight, with Rudolf Nureyev becoming 'artistic laureate' as well as dancing as a regular guest artist.

From 1987 until his death in 1998 the company was fortunate to have Christopher Gable as its artistic director. His career as a dancer with the Royal Ballet was followed by that of actor on stage as well as in film and television. He was thus able to focus as much on the 'theatre' as on the 'ballet' in the company's title, mounting such diverse full-length productions as *Swan Lake*, *The Brontes* and *Dracula*.

Christopher Gable gained the National Ballet Theatre a worldwide reputation. It has continued to go from strength to strength, notable events including the well-received adaptation of Dickens's *Great Expectations*, premiered in the company's home city of Leeds in February 2000. Yorkshire links continue to be emphasised by the current director David Nixon, whose first complete new work for NBT, *Wuthering Heights*, was described as 'a glorious collaboration' with the composer Claude-Michel Schönberg.

Chiaki Nagao in *Madame Butterfly*. (Brian Slater)

Desiré Samaai in *La Traviata*. (Brian Slater)

Christian Broomhall in *Peter Pan*. (Linda Rich)

Transformation accomplished. An August 2006 photograph looking down on the new and more spacious seating layout in the stalls of what is now known as the Yorkshire Bank Auditorium.

TRANSFORMATION

Lord Harewood made another and perhaps more telling comment at the time of the 2003 silver jubilee: 'Considering that Opera North has grown up and practised in a building which has been visibly decaying for all of the twenty-five years we have worked there, we have not done so badly.' It was a statement reflecting the fact that the Royal Opera House, the English National Opera at the Coliseum, Glyndebourne and Scottish Opera had all either built anew or restructured their existing buildings in recent times.

In contrast, Opera North suffered the major handicap that it owned no property. Many of its rehearsals took place in a small basement studio at the Grand or in rented accommodation in other parts of Leeds, with orchestral rehearsals consigned to a disused school on the outskirts of the city. Scenery storage was some nine miles away on an industrial estate adjacent to the motorways. Its main premises at the Grand fell well short of acceptable standards for staff and artists and compared unfavourably with those of similar companies. An additional drawback was that these premises were hidden away at the rear of the theatre and thus there was limited awareness in Leeds of the company's physical presence in the city. Lack of public access restricted the expansion of educational and similar work.

Truth to tell, although the Grand had in 1969 been saved from sudden death in the shape of demolition, there had down the years seldom been sufficient funds to ensure that it moved with the times. The expectations of both theatre and opera goers had moved on and facilities at the Grand were becoming increasingly outdated. The seating was almost impossibly cramped with the lack of an adequate rake from front to back creating acute visibility problems. Lack of space in the main theatre paled into insignificance when compared with the bars, where the scrum in gaining access was merely the forerunner of the greater challenge of getting served. Backstage the position was even more serious with performers describing the facilities as positively antiquated. The theatre had acquired a reputation as one of the most difficult in the country for mounting scenery, the overall result being that epic drama in the shape of the Royal Shakespeare Company and the National Theatre failed to materialise.

The expectations of both theatre and opera goers had moved on and facilities at the Grand were becoming increasingly outdated.

By the 1990s facilities at the Grand were becoming increasingly outdated. By modern standards the seating was 'almost impossibly cramped', as can be seen in this view of the closely packed tiers of seats in the upper circle. (YPN)

On its opening the Grand proudly boasted that it provided 'a perfect sightline from almost every seat'. Latter-day patrons have had their doubts, citing acute visibility problems caused by the lack of an adequate rake from front to back. Close study of the audience in this photograph suggests that many must have found their view obstructed. (YPN)

It was not just the audience who felt the facilities at the Grand were becoming outdated. Getting scenery and props in and out of the building posed considerable difficulties as seen here in April 1976. (YPN)

An official report concluded that the building itself had become 'demoted' in the streetscape due in part to the poor quality of the shop units and the general lack of 'spirit' and sense of arrival at the main entrance. Other theatres in the region, notably the Bradford Alhambra and the Sheffield Lyceum, had already successfully addressed similar problems and it was clear that the point had been reached where decisive action could be postponed no longer.

As it was also clear that this action had to be carefully measured. The Grand had at last been recognised as 'one of the finest survivals of Victorian theatre architecture in England', a conservation plan noting that it was hard to find anything – even in London – to compare with its 'opulence, complexity and scale'. In addition, the oft-quoted words of the distinguished American actor, Alfred Lund, still had a haunting presence: 'What a magnificent theatre! I hope nobody will ever be allowed to lay hands on it. A theatre like this cannot be improved. They got it right first time.'

An inspiring response to the many and various considerations evolved in the shape of the Transformation project, designed to 'transform' the Grand back to its former glory but also taking its name from the deeper concept that 'live theatre, opera and dance has the capacity to transform all our lives and even change our view of the world'. A partnership between the Grand Theatre, Opera North, Leeds City Council, Arts Council England and many others, it amounted to one of the largest arts building projects in the country with a cost estimated in 2000 at a figure of between £21 million and £25 million.

The overall aim of 'Transformation' was to restore and reveal the Theatre's splendid heritage and beauty while creating new technical facilities for visiting companies and a comfortable environment for audiences. Changes in the auditorium include new and refurbished seating, improved ventilation and air-conditioning, enhanced acoustics for both audience and performers, and improved access for people with disabilities. A deeper orchestra pit provides more player space and better access, while beyond the stage there are improved dressing rooms, a raised and upgraded scenery flying system and a hydraulic lorry lift providing access for even the most ambitious equipment.

Retention of the many and often little noticed features of the Grand's architecture has been a key priority in the conservation aspects of the Transformation project.

A typical example is this delightful stained glass window.

Victorian technology still in existence among the rafters.

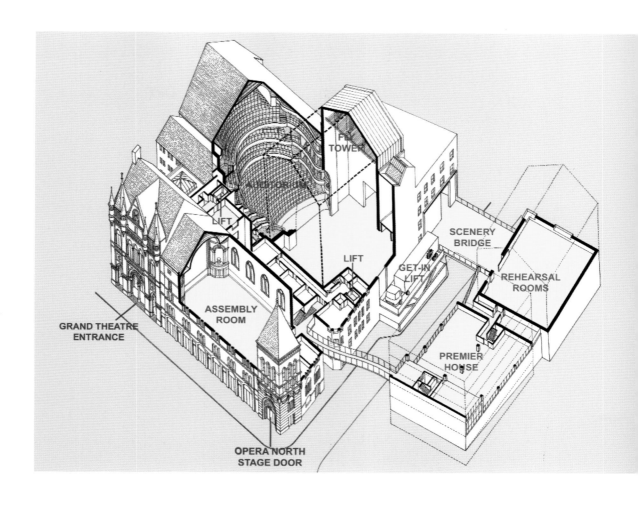

FLY
TOWER

AUDITORIUM

LIFT

LIFT

SCENERY
BRIDGE

GET-IN
LIFT

REHEARSAL
ROOMS

ASSEMBLY
ROOM

GRAND THEATRE
ENTRANCE

PREMIER
HOUSE

OPERA NORTH
STAGE DOOR

New technology. Installation of the hydraulic lorry lift, which will provide access to the theatre for equipment of virtually all shapes and sizes.

Artist's perspective of the transformed Grand Theatre & Opera House, with the entrance to the former Assembly Rooms on the right.

A second artist's perspective, showing in close up the former Assembly Rooms entrance and Harrison Street.

The 'Transformation' project covers the Grand Theatre & Opera House as a whole with all its ancillary buildings. These include the Assembly Rooms, which were converted into a pioneer cinema in 1912. When the doors of what had become the Plaza cinema closed in 1978, it was largely forgotten and most passers-by had little idea of the treasure that lay hidden behind the pollution-scarred entrance and grime-covered windows.

The new project embraces the restoration of the Assembly Rooms to create a 350-seat performance space with facilities for rehearsals, education workshops, showcasing new talent and for social and corporate entertaining.

Closure of the Plaza enabled the decorative and largely forgotten entrance to the former Assembly Rooms to be exposed to public view once more. Under the 'Transformation' project it will lead into a 350-seat performance space with many additional facilities. (Leodis Collection/Leeds Library and Information Services)

The former Assembly Rooms became a cinema as early as 1912. Changing its name to the Plaza in 1958, it rarely sought the cultural heights and at the time of this photograph in October 1975 its double-bill comprised *French Love* and *Sexy Lovers*. It was perhaps no surprise that the cinema closed three years later. (YPN)

Opera North – still the only 'mainscale' opera company in England outside London – is benefiting hugely from 'Transformation'. Instead of being spread across a number of buildings in and beyond the city, it is now seeing all its artistic development brought together on one site to create a centre of excellence with national impact. Richard Mantle, the company's General Director, explained at the outset: 'We open a new chapter with the prospect of new premises in which to work, perform and engage with new audiences. The opportunity at last to acquire a purpose-built home for our company, the first in our history, is a tantalising prospect. Alongside the Theatre we will create an integrated Opera Centre as the permanent home of Opera North, creating an environment in which a world-class opera company can experiment and flourish.'

Echoing sentiments expressed on the Grand Theatre's opening night in 1878, Lord Harewood commented: 'We in Leeds and the north of England deserve this. One of the curious things is that on the Continent public funding bodies are pretty good about dealing with what's necessary. Leeds is very slow over concert halls. That's a pity. Manchester has got one and Birmingham and Gateshead. Liverpool has had one for years. Why we should lag behind I don't know.'

The project got fully under way in October 2004 with the launching of the Transformation Fundraising Campaign, seeking to raise £5 million from individuals, local communities and companies towards the total cost of the project. Performances at the Grand continued until the end of May 2005 with *Blood Brothers* being chosen as the last production. The final evening was an emotional occasion with the General Manager, Warren Smith, echoing the theatre's opening night and giving a speech from the stage. His words recalled those of his predecessor Wilson Barrett in 1878, especially when he similarly referred to the fireproof nature of the Grand but nevertheless emphasised that the audience should 'please leave carefully'. Then the lights went out and it was the end of an era.

'We in Leeds and the north of England deserve this.' Lord Harewood

Willy Russell's *Blood Brothers* with its suitably emotional scenes formed the last production at the Grand before the lights went out and Transformation began.

The following weekend saw a special behind-the-scenes open day, which attracted some 4,500 visitors who were treated to full backstage tours. A group from Skipton Little Theatre succinctly recorded their impressions of the day: 'Down a flight, up a flight, round a corner, under the stage. The maze of backstage corridors and rooms was just as huge as the stage space itself. The theatre is a bit like an iceberg, with the auditorium and public rooms comprising only a fraction of the whole building. There are multiple dressing rooms, a large wardrobe room, corridors and offices galore, the paint frame where the scenery is created – the list goes on. We went into the Queen's loo, the Boardroom, the Lighting Control Rooms and the fly-walks, six stories up, from where the scenery is dropped down onto the stage.'

A highlight of the open day was an auction of surplus effects that raised £11,500, the items under the hammer being notable for their enormous variety and ranging from a golden fleece to a ram's head mask and a parasol from *Madame Butterfly* to programmes from past productions. There was brisk business in the sale of some 500 seats at £25 a throw, purchasers ranging from small theatre companies to individuals who simply wanted a memento of where they had placed their posterior to watch many a performance. A separate room allowed visitors to vote on their favourite style of new seat. On stage a memorabilia stall was busy all afternoon disposing of posters, photographs, costume pictures and design sketches. One visitor commented: 'They were trying to get money for old rope – literally, with coils of stage rigging rope for £3 each.'

Transformation underway in the auditorium with protective sheeting everywhere but many of the most distinctive features still recognisable.

The new era for the Grand, symbolised by the towering crane and the theatre – covered in scaffolding and protective sheeting – rising above the decorative pediments of a nearby building.

When it was all over, the contractors moved in and got to work with a vengeance on what was now a £31.5 million project funded by its main sponsors and no less than 40,000 individual donors. Despite past reports of theatre ghosts, including an apparition at the back of the dress circle wearing Cavalier-style costume, no skeletons or phantoms of the opera came to light. However, as walls were demolished a 'secret room' complete with its original gas fittings was found at the back of the stalls. Equally fascinating was the discovery under the stalls of programmes dating back to the First World War, still with the instruction to purchasers 'Please refuse if seal is broken'. This was a practice that lasted until 1971 and was designed to prevent theatre staff indulging in a profitable sideline by collecting programmes after a performance and re-selling them. Times have changed!

Silver shovels to the fore for the ceremonial start of construction work on the Transformation project in summer 2005

Such a huge project has inevitably attracted many interested visitors. These children have donned hard hats and have an audio aid to take round with them.

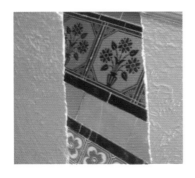

There have inevitably been some unexpected discoveries during the work, including some splendid 'period' tiles concealed behind heavily embossed wallpaper. Investigations have found that these dust-pressed encaustic tiles were made by W. Whetstone, Coalville.

View from on high looking straight down to the orchestra pit, which is being deepened as part of the project.

The results of 'Transformation', photographed in August 2006.

New seating in the stalls, with the revealed original tile work in the background.

Waterford Crystal chandelier suspended above the Yorkshire Bank Auditorium.

The new Harewood Rehearsal Studio of Opera North.

GRAND TOUR

Photographs illustrate far better than words just how difficult a balancing act has been required in bringing the Grand up to modern standards without destroying the period charm of its magnificent interior. Ian Grundy comprehensively photographed the theatre in 2003 prior to the start of 'Transformation'. Here is a selection of pictures, working from the entrance into the auditorium, with detailed views of many unique features ranging from fan vaulting to statues.

GRAND HALL

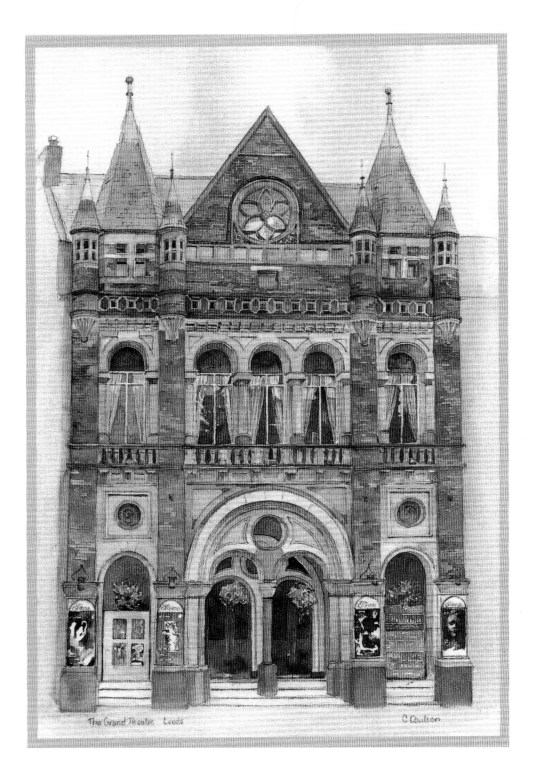

The Grand Theatre, Leeds

C Coulson

(painting by Carol Coulson)

GRAND MEMORIES

Prior to its temporary closure for refurbishment in 2005, the Grand Theatre issued an open invitation to the public to come inside for one last look before its 'Transformation'.

The management had the foresight to provide a book of memories at the open day in which visitors were asked to record their recollections of the theatre. The response to this request was far greater than anyone expected as people queued to provide personal reminiscences, stretching back from the present day to the 1920s. A selection of these memories is included in this chapter. One particular feeling expressed again and again is that the experience of first entering the Grand as a child remains a vivid memory that is re-kindled every time the theatre is revisited as an adult.

Margaret Barraclough, Rounday, Leeds

I was born in 1915 at Cemetery Road, Beeston, Leeds. My father, William Barraclough, was a self-employed theatrical advertising agent and represented many Leeds theatres in their heyday.

I first went to the Leeds Grand in 1920 when I vaguely remember the costumes in *Chu Chin Chow*. Then in 1922, when I still believed in fairies, I saw *Peter Pan* and was enchanted. Of course there were many pantomimes. In later years I saw Jack Tripp as a pantomime dame and thought he was the most charming, sparkling dame I had ever seen. About a year ago this was confirmed by two well-known actors, Lionel Blair and Roy Hudd.

In 1926 Arthur Riscoe and Cora Goffin were in *The Girl Friend*. They sang the lovely song, 'We'll have a blue room, a new room.' Another recollection is of Jack Buchanan and his leading lady Elsie Randolph in *That's a Good Girl*.

During the first year of the last war, Vivien Leigh came to the Grand in *Doctor's Dilemma*. I sat about six rows from the front of the orchestra stalls with binoculars and thought she was the most beautiful woman I had ever seen. The year before she was in the famous film, *Gone with the Wind*, with Clark Cable.

I have been thrilled and enchanted by many performances of glitter and glamour in a world of fantasy and make believe by many artists and celebrities.

Frank Readman, Scarborough

Earliest memory 1925, age five. My parents brought me to see the pantomime. We travelled from Whitby by train especially. Mother and I were in the balcony and father in the stalls. Norman Evans came off the stage in the interval and chatted to my father. I was in the balcony and could see but couldn't get down – I was quite annoyed!

Clifford Spark, Oxenhope

I have many memories of the Grand. I think I would make my first visit about 1928/30 to the pantomime with my parents. We would go for the evening performance and queue in the passage to the left of the main entrance. I think the price was two shillings and 'early doors' meant you had a choice of seats. We would sit in the theatre for what seemed to me a long time and then the Pit Stalls office would open and the rest of the Pit Stalls patrons would come in. They paid 1s 6d but we affluent customers had the best seats.

The yearly visit to the pantomime was the only visit as a child and the only name I can remember was Johnny Fuller. His speciality was playing the cat in *Dick Whittington* and the whole of the time he was on stage he was on all fours. During the interval, he would come out and walk around the edge of the dress circle. You can imagine what Health and Safety would have thought about the interval performance.

I also remember one production of *Faust*. It was during the war and the chorus was composed of elderly ladies and gentlemen. There was also an economic restraint on numbers so you can imagine the Soldiers' Chorus! Eight or ten elderly men marching in single file across the stage, running round the back and re-emerging to repeat the process. They began very 'forte' but by the end they had run out of puff and it became rather 'pianissimo'.

Evelyn Sarvent, Leeds

Earliest memory 1932. Pantomime with Cora Goffin as principal boy. Always enjoyed singing along during pantomimes when the words were let down on a huge sheet, especially:

> *Never let your braces dangle*
> *Dingle, dingle, dangle*
> *One old sport, he got caught*
> *Right into the mangle.*
> *Right through the rollers he went by gum*
> *Came out flat as linoleum*
> *Now he's singing in kingdom come*
> *Never let you braces come undone.*

First sat in the upper balcony ('gods') for ninepence. There was great excitement each time we queued – early doors – for the gods and then the long climb up the stairs. We were often asked to push up further along the benches – that was before tip-up seats were in place there.

Rose Green (nee Harrison), Leeds

I appeared in *Robinson Crusoe*, Christmas 1933 to March 1934, as a member of the chorus. Elsie Prince was principal boy and Barry Lupino was the dame. Ten local girls were chosen each year to work with the London girls. I received three shillings per show.

Rose Green (nee Harrison) pictured in January 1934 in her Grand Finale costume for Robinson Crusoe.

The refurbished auditorium, photographed in August 2006 from the stage. The view looks up to the 'gods' (the upper balcony), where Evelyn Sarvent paid ninepence to sit on benches in the days before tip-up seats. Progress has come a long way!

Ann Smith

I look back on many Grand Theatre visits: Flora Robson in The Innocents; Robert Morley in The Little Hut; great performances by Dame Edith Evans, and John Reed; opera singers Rita Hunter and James Johnstone; ballet with Margot Fonteyn and Rudolf Nureyev. There were comedians Arthur Askey, Norman Evans and Nat Jackley, and pantomime greats such as Evelyn Laye (who, as a Principal Boy in sparkling silver lamé armour, kissed my hand when as a small girl I sat in the stage box above the orchestra!).

Amusing incidents come to mind, such as the theatre cat crossing the darkened stage behind the lone mezzo soprano singing the tragic aria from Act 3 of Carmen, the poor singer unable to understand the titters from the audience; likewise the witch in Hansel and Gretel unable to rise into the air on her broomstick as the 'flying' mechanism had stuck.

Sheila Verity

When Noel Coward and Gertrude Lawrence appeared in Tonight at 8.30 every seat was taken and many people were standing at the back of the stalls. Productions were often tried out in the provinces before opening in London – some were successful, others not. James Mason came in a play, long before he became famous.

Eric Mountain

I remember the premiere of Expresso Bongo with Paul Schofield. On the first night a prop fireplace fell over and with perfect timing he walked across the stage, picked it up and leaned against it while a stagehand nipped on and braced it back in position. Not a line was missed!

Tom Webb

Before the war all the great stars of theatre came to the Grand – Richard Burton in his first role in The Lady's not for Burning, Noel Coward, Gertrude Lawrence, the wonderful musicals of Ivor Novello and visits by the Carl Rosa Opera Company and Sadler's Wells.

We queued for the Pit Stalls and entered in single file through a very narrow passageway. I believe the Pit then consisted of padded forms, later replaced by seats.

Mavis Hoyles, Bramley, Leeds

Earliest memory 1935 Christmas pantomime. I came with my mum and dad and we queued up for seats in the upper balcony. It felt like we were climbing up to heaven.

In 1944 I came with a school party to see John Gielgud in *Macbeth* in preparation for school certificate examinations. I saw *Swan Lake* sometime between 1985 and 1990. It was the first time that I had been to a ballet and I persuaded my husband to come along too. We were both converted.

Mavis Unsworth, Leeds

Earliest memory July 1940 for my birthday. My mother had booked a box for my friends and us. Very excited but no idea what we saw – couldn't have been *Peter Pan* could it or was that at The Royal?

In late 1980s saw *Henry IV* parts 1 and 2 and *Henry V.* In one day we saw three plays. Michael Pennington was Hal then Henry. It was wonderful and well worth the "numb bum" after sitting for nine hours. The seats were comfortable but not that comfortable!

Doreen Taylor (nee Brewerton), Cleckheaton

I have wonderful memories of the Leeds Grand Theatre as I met my future husband there. We met in a show called *Youth Marches On!* I was in the Girl Guides aged fifteen, he was in the Boys' Brigade aged seventeen. The show ran for a week in June 1945 and included Brownies, Scouts and lots more. What lovely memories even though it was a long time ago.

Meg Cawthorne, Batley

Earliest memory 1945. I lived in a small village between Pontefract and Goole called Hensall. We only came to Leeds once a year to see the pantomime. I was really convinced that the flying fairies were real. But during one interval when I was about ten, I asked my mum what the wires were that were attached to the sides of the upper circle. She shattered my childhood completely when she told me they were to hold the fairies up and I got told off for being upset.

I come to everything – plays, musicals, opera and ballet – and I let my mind wander back to that time when I felt so hurt to find out those fairies were not real.

Peter Perkin, Pudsey

I started my musical career at this theatre in 1946, taking lessons from Harold V Smith who was a drummer in the Grand Orchestra. Many of my lessons were held either in the 'pit' or the grand hall. Around 1976, I was in the orchestra when Pudsey Grammar School gave a production of *Doctor's Orders.*

The 'Camp Fire' scene in the June 1945 production of *Youth Marches On!* This view may well include Doreen Brewerton, then a Girl Guide aged fifteen, as it was on this occasion that she met her future husband – a seventeen-year-old member of the Boys' Brigade.
(Leodis Collection/YPN)

Carole Baker, Addingham

Earliest memories 1947-53 (every year around my birthday). Each year, my father's works outing came to the pantomime at the Grand. I never failed to be thrilled as the curtain was raised and the lights came up on the opening chorus full of colour and dancing men, women and children. I have that feeling to this day.

Margaret Edwards-Smith, Menston

Special occasion – Easter 1948. On the day of my engagement, we bought the ring, had lunch, then saw an Ivor Novello play – *Magical* – from the Dress Circle.

Merel Jackson (nee Wood), Leeds

I recall my first visit backstage at the Grand Theatre. I was nineteen years old and a member of Leeds Amateur Operatic Society, doing *Show Boat*, the Diamond Jubilee celebration in 1950. In between rehearsing, we explored the whole of the backstage and front of house. There were still some gas lights in the corridor and plain concrete floors and stairs. It was a most striking experience. I was wide-eyed with amazement and shall never forget the enjoyment and friendship of the LAOS, which started at the Grand Theatre.

Audrey Cornell, Morley

I have many happy memories from the early 1950s of Tuesday matinees with my grandmother at half term when I was introduced to John Hanson's repertoire, which widened my musical taste. I've stood at the back of the stalls with my mum on a Saturday night to watch the likes of *Salad Days* because all the seats were sold out.

In my teens, I even 'trod the boards' myself as a Leeds Thespian. I ventured backstage many years later to help chaperone the babes in *Babes in the Wood* with the late Les Dawson – a lovely man. I think Wyn Calvin was the dame and the Dallas Boys were the robbers.

I can remember standing in the street opposite about forty years ago to watch the Queen arrive one evening to watch Handel's *Samson*. So many wonderful memories!

John Gasgoigne, Doncaster

It was February 1954 – *Robinson Crusoe*. I was eleven years old and this trip to the theatre was the culmination of the Coronation celebrations the previous year for all the kids, and some grown ups too, from my village. This was a special occasion. I will never forget my first memories of the theatre itself. A big chandelier, the orchestra, the atmosphere, it was magic. Whenever I step into the theatre, it is still exciting just as it was then.

Barbara Gledhill, Leeds

Earliest memories 1956 to 1958. My younger sister and myself went to the theatre with my aunt and uncle. We always sat in a box. I remember feeling like a princess especially at the interval when the waitress arrived carrying a silver tray with coffees and ice creams for us all.

Rowena Harker Leder

The Grand in Leeds has been my major theatre all my life and this must be the same for most people of my age (almost 70 years) living in the north of England. It has always been there as the most exciting destination when leaving Grassington for a special treat. I can still see myself as a small girl leaning over the edge of the Dress Circle box, closest to the stage, and Norman Evans stared up at me and called out 'Mind the plush!' The whole theatre looked up and I shrivelled back into my seat.

The Grand Theatre staff seemed to be a race apart. The ushers and ticket sales people have always been helpful and friendly and the greatest accolade goes to the helpers in the Grand Hall. The early suppers provided for the Friends of Opera North have been a great delight over the years. To leave Grassington soon after 5.30pm, fly over the moors to Leeds, park easily because of being early and then have a relaxed supper and study the programme, was always a perfect evening.

The Grand Theatre is a monument in the north and loved and needed by anyone and everyone who cares about music and performance. Its renovation is long overdue and greatly appreciated.

Mike Crosfill, Leeds

Earliest memory 1957 pantomime. Also recall seeing David Essex, Hot Chocolate, Hollies, Leo Sayer and *Hair*. Favourite show – Elton John's Rocket Show. A superb show. First time we saw Elton John. Came down without a ticket. Asked doorman to keep ears open for two tickets. Thirty minutes before the show, two tickets came up. Front row of dress circle for face value £3.

Gillian Batty, Garforth

It was in the 1950s and I was about three or four. I came to see a pantomime starring David Whitfield and sat in the front row of the stalls with my grandparents. During the show he came down to the orchestra by the conductor's desk. He asked me to come and sit by his side. I remember the spotlight shining very brightly in my face. He said I had beautiful blue eyes and felt sorry for the people in the audience who wouldn't get a chance to see them! He asked me whom I loved most. "My Daddy," I replied. He then sang 'Daddy's Little Girl' to me. I loved it and because I had been so good he presented me with a posy. It was gorgeous. Even today, I cannot look at anemones without thinking of my wonderful experience at the theatre.

Eileen Crosfill

Earliest memory 1959 pantomime. I also remember seeing *Hair*, famous for its controversial nude scene. I didn't tell anyone for years that I had seen it!

Mrs Ryder, Leeds

In 1959 I came to see Bruce Forsyth. I was celebrating my birthday and visited him in his dressing room with some friends and gave him a piece of birthday cake.

Jesamy Robinson, Bradford

Earliest memory 1960. Works outing to the pantomime followed by fish and chip supper at Harry Ramsdens with my mother and sister. Also saw Morecambe and Wise and Tommy Cooper.

Beryl Sidwell, Wakefield

Earliest memory about 1970. *Ride, Ride* – the story of John Wesley's life, riding on horseback around the country. For the whole week my youth club was involved in selling programmes – we dressed in 18th century costumes. It was the only time I have seen the dressing rooms and backstage. Having seen every performance, the theme song 'Riding for the Lord' is well and truly lodged in my memory. It was a wonderful experience for a fairly local Methodist. A week I cheerfully took part in and will always remember.

Gillian Bell, Leeds

Special occasion – pantomime 1962. I was a sunbeam in *Sleeping Beauty* with David Whitfield, Morecambe and Wise and Patricia Lambert. Ernie Wise had a black Scottish terrier. David Whitfield gave me a silver threepenny bit.

Mollie Falkiner, Leeds

Special occasion – 1962. This was my twenty-first birthday. We booked the Royal Box at each side of the stage to see David Whitfield and Morecambe and Wise. I have the ticket stub – £4 8s 0d each box. David Whitfield sang to me.

Philip Booth, Pontefract

First performed here in October 1965 with the Operatic Society. Did twelve shows and worked here as a dresser. I remember the theatre before it had alterations to below stage and ruined the place. I recall an old man that remembered gas footlights.

I G McLean, Leeds

Earliest memory 1969-70. School trip to see *Richard II* for A Level English Literature. Robert Powell was the lead and all the girls had a crush on him.

Favourite show – Dave Allan, late 1980s or early 1990s. One-man show by this great artist. When he came on for the second half, he gave a drink to a lady in a box 'whiskey,' she said, which echoed round the theatre.

Margaret Ashbee, Marketing Department, The Grand

On a school trip in the late 1960s or early 1970s I came to see *The Winslow Boy* with Richard Todd. I got his autograph after the show. I can remember coming for my interview in July 1994 and spending ages figuring out how to get into the building! I still think that the stage door is hard to find until you know where it is.

Carol Clark, Leeds

Earliest memory 1975-ish. I played cousin Hebe in *HMS Pinafore*. It was a school production and I will never forget walking out onto the stage. I also did various productions with Leeds Thespians.

Olav Arnold

In 1976 the Ring came to Leeds Grand. Performances of all the four operas were given by English National Opera conducted by Reginald Goodall, the doyen of Wagner opera conductors. It was performed in English and we collected a group of about eight friends to go every night. Supper was organised in the long interval at local restaurants in Merrion Street and the meal ordered for the specific time scheduled (it was not always ready!), so that we could eat our mixed grill or the like and get back in time for the second half.

We were immersed in Wagner's music for the whole week and it dominated our lives for a brief period. I wonder if it will happen again?

Alison Davis, Bradford

First came in the 1980s. Favourite show – *The Play What I Wrote*. During the performance, the lead actor threw a rubber duck into the audience and I caught it. On the duck was written, 'I am not supposed to be out here, please leave me on your seat and I will be collected by the crew.' I've a picture taken with the duck!

Mrs Rock, Ilkley

I shall never forget the occasion when the Duke of Kent attended the opera at the Grand Theatre. The audience were settling down to enjoy the start of the opera when the orchestra suddenly began to play the National Anthem. The audience sprang to its feet in various degrees of shock and unpreparedness!

Linda Hepworth, Leeds

Favourite show – 1995 *Rocky Horror Show*. A group of ten of us had been avid fans of the show since its beginning. We didn't have to dress up because we were Goths and naturally fitted in.

Sue Thorp

June 2002. I have so many happy memories of performing with Sing Live Northern in *Evita*. We had a wonderful time and played to packed houses – not bad for amateurs. My personal claim to fame was a walk-on part as the nursemaid to the dying 'Eva' where I tidied her hair prior to her final press call, then tried not to cry as she 'passed away'. Sir Tim Rice came to our last performance and was full of praise. Happy memories indeed!

Corinne Batty, Garforth

Earliest memory 2002. The show was *Grease*. I came to see it with my local youth group. I loved the show – it was full of energy. The actors were superb. I'm not old enough to have many memories of the Grand, but hopefully when the theatre is restored I can create new memories of wonderful acts and shows.

Several children recorded their recollections in the book of memories complete with coloured drawings. Above is the contribution of Olivia June Portman of Grange Moor, Wakefield, now age nine, who depicted her impression of seeing *Romeo and Juliet* when she was six.

Below, Harvey Thurwell of Methley, now eight, went to see *Joseph and the Amazing Technicolor Dreamcoat* when he was five.

SOMETHING WAS DIFFERENT THAT NIGHT

Sir Thomas Allen

It seems as though fate has finally played a part in my writing about a memory of the Grand Theatre after almost thirty-five years. Certainly something occurred then, of which those who were performing were aware, and which has caused me to wonder over the years whether anyone who was present that night also sensed a special 'happening'.

I was on tour with Welsh National Opera appearing in a new production of Billy Budd, Benjamin Britten's great opera. It had been well received a season before at its premiere in Cardiff, but the regard then for this opera was not what it is now. Indeed, at times we felt as though we were involved in musical missionary work, trying to find audiences for what was, and to some extent still is, regarded as a controversial work.

Here we were in Leeds on its opening night of a short season. Michael Geliot, director of the production, was there, and perhaps even Roger Butlin, its designer. James Lockhart, the company's music director, conducted. Some of the cast are no longer with us: Bryan Drake, John Gibbs and Forbes Robinson – the most menacing of John Claggarts. Nigel Douglas was Captain Vere.

We knew one another well from previous performances and of course the lengthy rehearsal period. All the same personnel then, and the same chorus and orchestra. But something was different that night.

I'm not sure whether it made its presence felt during the show, but certainly at the final curtain we knew to a man that we had experienced something very rare in the theatre.

Vere sang his last words, "When I, Edward Fairfax Vere, commanded the Indomitable..."

And then – silence. A silence that seemed to go on and on for minutes and yet was probably no more than eight seconds or ten seconds at most.

Applause began to seep in quietly, the curtain having now descended. No infuriating 'clappus interruptus' as I like to think of it on this occasion, that all too well known sign from someone anxious to let us all know – should we need it – that the show is over and he knows better than anyone.

But not this time, not on this evening. The atmosphere was religious in its intensity.

And on stage. The heartiness of a crew, all fully paid up members of Equity, absent now. Instead, just a respectful line up of subdued people at the end of a disturbing night's work.

The curtain opened and we acknowledged the applause that now came to us in great waves. But even then there was no great celebration. We took our quiet leave of one another, went to our dressing rooms, washed off and went home through the wet Leeds night.

I think there are still those about who remember that performance. On occasion I remember a few of us referring to it as though a great landmark in our lives. Perhaps it was. Certainly such moments come along but rarely. On reflection that is just as well.

There is no explanation for them – those strange unaccountable evenings. The chemistry, the planets – who knows?

An experience worth having though. If ever one entertained doubts about the efficacy of drama – and musical drama in particular – a night like that at the Grand Theatre thirty-five years ago scotched all that.

Grand Theatre - Leeds.

SUBSCRIBERS

John Adams

Christopher Ainslie

Richard Allison

Margaret Barraclough

R H & M M Barraclough

Mr W A Baugh

Donald Bedford

Jean Birdsall

Mr C Blackwell

Mr Henry Boot

Milton Booth

Keith Clasper Borthwick

Peter & Pat Boyes

Sylvia Bradburn

Pat Bruce

Hazel & Jeffrey Burns

Edith Carrigill

Lynda Susan Cheney

David & Mary Clarkson

Pamela Constable

Rita Croft

L Crosland

Mr L Crosland

John S Dawson

Frank Dodsworth

Philip Duffy

Gail Dyson

Susan May Eastwood

Ronald Ellis

Graham Fatorinni

Mr Ralph Firth

Desmond Fitzgerald

Frank "Frisky" Fletcher

Mr & Mrs Trevor Ford

Hon. Ald. D E Gabb

Michael Gager

Winifred Gaunt

Ann Garnett

Ian D Geldart

Sidney Gordon

Rose Green

Ruth Hamilton-Rudd

Martin Handley

Dorothy Haxby

Henry Heyworth

Christopher Hiley

J Holmes

Allan House

Marian Impey

Don James

Elizabeth Johnson

Susan Jones

Maureen Kershaw

Elaine Barbara King

Mr & Mrs Robert Lawrence

Andy Lightfoot

Mr Arthur Liley

Miss M Lound

Graham Lunn

Maureen Mackie

Alan Makinson

Chris Marks

Michael Matthews

Alec & Edith McLean

Terence Stephen Meegan

John Lawrence Midgley

Colin Mitchell

Leslie Mitchell

Irene Naylor

D Osborne

T Parkinson

B & P Remington

John & Stella Rigby

Dave & Christine Scholes

Mr & Mrs Seaman

Mrs C D Seipp

Donald Senior

J R Shenton

Christine Mary Smith

Derek Smith

Rosemary K Smith

Irene Stainburn

David Steadman

Eric & June Stephenson

F R A Stirk

Mo Stokes

Richard T Strudwick

Liz Summers

Gerald Tatham

Stephanie Thompson

Denis Brook & Linda Townend

Doreen Tring

Granville Roy Wagstaff

Moira Walker

Ian J Ward (Thorner)

Shirley Royce Wareing

Margaret R Watson

Elaine Whitaker

Helen White

Elizabeth Whitehead

Frank & Sheila Whitelow

Eric Wild

Leslie & Barbara Wilson

Andrew Keith Wood

Lara Woodhouse

Nancy Wooler

Helen Wright